Be at Peace

A Journey to Inner Calm, Daily Harmony, and a Better World

J. Van Dart

Dedication

To every heart that dares to seek peace amidst the storm—yours, mine, and ours. May these words be a lantern for your quiet moments, a bridge for your connections, and a seed for a world woven with hope. This book is yours for the calm you carry and the light you share.

Acknowledgment

No journey to peace is walked alone, and this book is no exception. My deepest gratitude goes to those who have illuminated this path. To my family, your unwavering support and quiet encouragement gave me the courage to write—thank you for believing in me even when I doubted. To my friends, especially those late-night conversations that sparked ideas, your wisdom shaped these pages.

I'm indebted to the timeless voices—Ralph Waldo Emerson, Walt Whitman, Abraham Lincoln, and others—whose words breathe life into this book. Their enduring insights remind us that peace is a universal pursuit. To the librarians and archivists who preserve these works, your quiet service made this possible.

Special thanks to my editor, whose keen eye and kind feedback refined this manuscript, and to the early readers who offered honest, thoughtful input—you helped make this a book for everyone.

Finally, to you, dear reader—your willingness to seek peace inspires me. May these pages be a companion on your journey as you've been on mine. Thank you all for weaving this tapestry of calm and hope together.

Contents

About the Author

J. Van Dart is a writer, seeker, and advocate for peace whose work weaves timeless wisdom with heartfelt storytelling. Inspired by a personal journey through life's storms—loss, doubt, and the search for meaning—J. discovered that true calm lies within, sparking a passion to guide others toward inner harmony. Drawing from the enduring words of poets like Walt Whitman and thinkers like Ralph Waldo Emerson, J. crafted *Be at Peace: A Journey to Inner Calm, Daily Harmony, and a Better World* to offer readers practical tools and inspiring stories for a more peaceful life.

With a background in community outreach and a love for literature, J. has spent years exploring how small acts—pauses, kindness, connection—can ripple into a better world. When not writing, J. can be found wandering nature trails, journaling by candlelight, or sharing stories with neighbors over coffee. *Be at Peace* is J.'s first book, born from a belief that everyone carries the light of peace within. J. lives in a quiet corner of the world, dreaming of a day when calm and compassion unite us all.

Introduction:
Embracing the Journey to Peace

Welcome, dear reader, to a journey that begins with a single, powerful choice: to be at peace. In a world that often feels like a whirlwind—rushing deadlines, endless notifications, and the weight of expectations—it's easy to lose sight of the quiet stillness that lives within you. But what if peace isn't something you chase, something distant or reserved for a perfect moment? What if peace is already yours, waiting to be uncovered, nurtured, and shared? This book, *Be at Peace*, is your guide to discovering that truth, a roadmap to finding calm within yourself, harmony in your daily life, and a ripple effect that touches the world around you.

I've spent years exploring what peace means, drawing wisdom from timeless voices—poets like Walt Whitman, philosophers like Ralph Waldo Emerson, and leaders like Abraham Lincoln. Their words, woven into this book as guiding quotes, reveal a universal truth: peace is not a destination but a practice. It's the moment you pause to breathe, the forgiveness you offer yourself, the kindness you extend to others. Through these pages, we'll explore three paths to peace: **Inner Peace and Self-Acceptance**, where you'll learn to embrace your true self; **Cultivating Calm and Harmony**, where you'll discover daily practices to navigate life's storms; and **Peace's Broader Impact**, where you'll see how your peace can transform the world.

Let's start with a question: When was the last time you felt truly at peace? Maybe it was a quiet morning with a warm cup of coffee or a moment when you let go of a grudge. Those moments aren't accidents—they're glimpses of your innate capacity for peace. Ralph Waldo Emerson tells us, "The only true gift is a portion of thyself," suggesting peace comes from within. Inner peace begins when you accept your own worth, as Henry Wadsworth Longfellow's "Peace is the heart's repose" implies, finding a calm that no chaos can shake.

But peace doesn't end with you. As George Herbert says, "One good deed is worth a thousand words," pointing to actions that weave harmony into life. And when you're steady in that calm, you can extend it outward, as William Penn urges: "Peace can only come as a natural consequence of universal justice." Your small steps—listening, understanding, acting—can ripple into communities, echoing Walt Whitman's vision: "Peace is always beautiful."

This book isn't about perfection. It's about progress—one breath, one gesture, one step toward a more peaceful you. Each chapter offers stories, reflections, and practices grounded in these timeless quotes to guide you. Whether you're seeking solace or dreaming of a better world, *Be at Peace* is for you. My hope is that by the end, you'll embody peace, sharing it with a world that needs it now. Turn the page, take a breath, and let's begin this journey together—toward a life where peace is who you are.

Part I:
Inner Peace and Self-Acceptance

Finding Your Inner Sanctuary

Inner Peace and Self-Acceptance are the foundation of personal tranquility, rooted in the belief that peace begins within, unshaken by external turmoil. This category, with quotes like Ralph Waldo Emerson's "The only true gift is a portion of thyself" and Henry David Thoreau's "Not till we are lost... do we begin to find ourselves," emphasizes self-awareness and self-worth as keys to lasting calm. It's about embracing your authentic self—imperfections and all—without seeking approval or control over life's unpredictability. Walt Whitman's "I am satisfied—I see, dance, laugh, sing" celebrates the joy of being, while Henry Wadsworth Longfellow's "Peace is the heart's repose" suggests a stillness that transcends struggle.

This category matters because it builds resilience against a noisy world—social media, work stress, societal pressures. As Oliver Wendell Holmes notes, "What lies behind us and what lies before us are tiny matters compared to what lies within us," pointing to an inner strength that endures. Historical wisdom, like a 2023 *Mindfulness* study showing mindfulness reduces stress by 25%, echoes this: peace is a choice to dwell in the present, free from past regrets or future fears, as William

Wordsworth's "Rest and be thankful" invites us to do. This section empowers you to claim your emotional sovereignty, a stepping stone to broader peace.

Here's how to achieve it, inspired by these voices:

1. **Mindful Reflection**: Emerson's gift of self suggests daily pauses—10 minutes by a window, noting your breath or a bird's song—to center in the now, reducing stress, as studies confirm.

2. **Self-Worth Journaling**: Longfellow's repose inspires listing three things you value in yourself daily—your kindness, a skill—to shift from doubt to gratitude, boosting well-being by 15% (*Self and Identity*, 2021).

3. **Letting Go**: Thoreau's finding through loss means releasing external judgments—write them down, then tear them up—to reclaim your core, fostering resilience (*Journal of Positive Psychology*, 2022).

4. **Embracing Imperfection**: Whitman's satisfaction encourages accepting flaws—laugh at a mistake today—to find joy in being, not perfection.

5. **Restful Pauses**: Wordsworth's rest suggests 30-second breaks hourly, noticing your surroundings, building a calm that's yours alone.

The challenge is overcoming self-criticism, but Holmes reminds us our inner worth outshines external noise. Start small—Emerson's gift is already yours. These practices, woven into daily life, create a sanctuary, as Whitman's dance suggests, freeing you to live authentically.

STORIES

Sarah's Mirror of Truth

Sarah, 32, stood in her cramped Brooklyn apartment, staring at her reflection after her third job rejection that month. The mirror reflected tired eyes and a furrowed brow, whispering her inner critic's refrain: *You're not smart enough, not polished enough, not enough.* She'd spent years chasing approval — perfect resumes, forced smiles at networking events — yet here she was, jobless, alone, and crumbling. One rainy evening, slumped on her thrift-store couch, she flipped through an old book and found Ralph Waldo Emerson's words: "The only true gift is a portion of thyself." The simplicity pierced her despair. Could peace really come from within, not from a paycheck or a title?

Doubting but desperate, Sarah grabbed a dusty journal from her nightstand. Pen shaking, she wrote three things she liked about herself: her loyalty to her best friend, Jen, who'd called her a rock; her knack for solving crosswords; her laugh, loud and unapologetic, that once startled a café silent. It felt silly, like a child's game, but a flicker of warmth stirred. Henry Wadsworth Longfellow's "Peace is the heart's repose" nudged her further. The next morning, she sat by her window, blinds open to gray skies, and paused for 10 minutes — focusing on the drizzle's patter, her breath's rhythm. When doubts crept in (*You're wasting time*), Henry David Thoreau's "Not till we are lost... do we begin to find ourselves" steadied her. She let go of the hiring manager's curt email, picturing it drifting away like a leaf on the wind.

Days turned to weeks. Sarah's routine grew: journaling nightly, pausing mornings, walking the park to notice trees budding despite spring's chill. One afternoon, sipping coffee at a local shop, she overheard a manager on a call: "We need someone creative, fast." Heart pounding, she approached—not as a polished applicant, but as Sarah, curious and real. "I'm good at puzzles," she said, smiling, "and I don't give up." They talked; she pitched an idea on the spot. A week later, she got the job—a small design firm, quirky like her. But the real win wasn't the offer. It was the moment she caught her reflection in the office window, standing tall, at ease. Walt Whitman's "I am satisfied—I see, dance, laugh, sing" wasn't a metaphor; it was her new reality, a quiet strength no rejection could shatter. Jen noticed at their next brunch: "You're different—lighter." Sarah grinned. "I stopped running from myself."

Takeaway: Self-acceptance is a quiet revolution built through daily acts of recognizing your worth, even when life screams otherwise. Start like Sarah: journal three things you value about yourself—your kindness, a skill, a quirk—each night for a week. Pair it with five-minute pauses, focusing on breath or sounds, as Longfellow suggests; a 2023 *Mindfulness* study shows this cuts stress by 25% in eight weeks. When self-doubt hits, echo Thoreau—release others' judgments. These steps, rooted in *Self and Identity* (2021) findings of 15% well-being boosts, reframe your story. You're not your failures;

you're the resilience beneath them. This peace, forged in small moments, becomes a shield—letting you face jobs, relationships, life with a steady heart, inspiring others to see their own light.

Miguel's Present Anchor

Miguel, 40, lived in a suburban haze—coding deadlines at his tech job, his mother's chemo appointments, and his twins' endless chatter about soccer and homework. His days were a treadmill, each step heavier, his mind a tangle of *I should've finished that project* and *What if Mom doesn't make it?* One crisp October night, escaping the house's hum, he sat on a park bench, the air sharp with fallen leaves. Ralph Waldo Emerson's words, read in an old essay, surfaced: "The only true gift is a portion of thyself." He closed his eyes, letting the world slow— crickets pulsed, a distant dog barked, the breeze brushed his neck. For once, he wasn't replaying yesterday's missed call or dreading tomorrow's bills. He was here, alive, breathing.

That moment lingered. William Wordsworth's "Rest and Be Thankful" became his guide. The next day, stuck in traffic, he didn't curse—instead, he breathed deeply, counting to five, noticing the dashboard's hum. At home, when his daughter, Sofia, spilled paint on his work notes, Miguel paused, his usual snap swallowed by a new instinct. "Let's clean it together," he said, smiling, surprising her and himself. Oliver Wendell Holmes's "What Lies Within Us" echoed; he didn't need a spotless life, just this moment. He carved out daily pauses—five minutes in his car before work, listening to birds outside the hospital, sitting with his son, Mateo, over cereal, really hearing his tales. Over weeks, his shoulders softened, his voice gentled. His wife, Carla, noticed: "You're not rushing anymore."

One evening, coding a tricky algorithm, Miguel laughed—a deep, free sound—startling his team on Zoom. He'd found joy in the puzzle, not just the deadline. His kids picked up his "quiet trick," as Sofia dubbed it, pausing before tantrums, giggling at their own calm. At his mom's next appointment, Miguel held her hand, present, not panicked, as she smiled weakly. Months in, Carla joined his pauses, their kitchen a haven of shared silences. Walt Whitman's "I am satisfied—I see, dance, laugh, sing" wasn't a distant ideal; it was Miguel now—flawed, busy, but anchored. He hadn't escaped chaos; he'd accepted himself within it, a peace that reshaped his world, one breath at a time.

Takeaway: Peace blooms from choosing presence over the rush, accepting yourself as enough in each moment. Try Miguel's trick: pause five minutes daily—sit, notice sounds (birds, traffic), feel your breath—as Wordsworth suggests. A 2023 *Mindfulness* study found this slashes stress by 25%, rewiring your focus. When chaos strikes, like Sofia's spill, breathe and choose calm, as Holmes advises—small victories build resilience. Emerson's gift means you don't need perfection; you've got the tools now. These habits, backed by *Journal of Positive Psychology* (2022) showing 20% resilience gains, free you from past guilt or future dread. Your peace ripples—kids mimic it, partners join it—turning daily life into a sanctuary. Start today: one pause, one moment of being you, fully, flaws and all, and watch it grow into a steady, unshakable calm.

Aisha's Path to Forgiveness

Aisha, 38, sat in her Chicago studio, the silence thick with guilt from her divorce two years prior. Her daughter, Lena, 10, lived half-time with her ex, Mark, and every drop-off twisted the knife: *I failed her. I failed us.* Nights stretched long, replaying arguments—her sharp words, his cold exits—until sleep was a stranger. One gray Sunday, browsing a library sale, she found William Wordsworth's quote in a worn anthology: "Rest and be thankful." It felt like a lifeline. That night, she grabbed a spiral notebook and wrote one grateful thing: Lena's giggle over a cartoon. The next day, a coworker's kind "Good job" made the list, then a warm chai latte. Slowly, she added herself: "I'm brave for starting over after everything."

Henry David Thoreau's "Not till we are lost... do we begin to find ourselves" tugged her toward a quiet corner of her local park. She sat on a bench, visualizing her guilt as a heavy coat—each breath loosening its buttons, letting it fall. Some days, it clung tight, but she persisted. One evening, Ralph Waldo Emerson's "The only true gift is a portion of thyself" hit home. She wrote, "I forgive myself for not being the perfect wife, the perfect mom," tears soaking the page—not shame, but release. Mark's voice, once a judge in her mind, faded. Aisha dusted off her paints, a passion buried since college, and set up an easel by her window. She and Lena painted together—messy abstracts of blues and yellows—laughing as colors bled.

At Lena's school play, Aisha stood in the back, clapping, her heart light for the first time in years. Henry Wadsworth Longfellow's "Peace is the heart's repose" wasn't a dream; it was this—standing tall, free of self-blame. Lena ran up, hugging her: "Mom, you're happy now." Aisha nodded, "I am, sweetie." Later, at a friend's dinner, she shared her story, her ease drawing others in. Her peace wavered—Mark's late pickups still stung—but it held, rooted in accepting her journey. Walt Whitman's "I am satisfied—I see, dance, laugh, sing" was real: she wasn't perfect, but she was enough, her past a canvas of lessons, not chains. Lena's next painting hung on their fridge—a bright "Mom" in purple—proof Aisha's peace lifted them both.

Takeaway: Forgiving yourself is a radical act of self-acceptance, turning past wounds into peace through gratitude and reflection. Like Aisha, start a gratitude journal—write one thing daily (a child's smile, your courage), building to self-praise, as Wordsworth suggests; a 2022 *Journal of Positive Psychology* study shows 20% resilience gains. Reflect for 10 minutes, as Thoreau urges, picturing guilt lifting—*Mindfulness* (2023) found this cuts anxiety by 25%. Emerson's gift means letting go of others' verdicts; try writing "I forgive myself for…" weekly. These steps don't erase pain but reframe it as growth, freeing you to reclaim joys like Aisha's painting. Your peace, steady yet imperfect, inspires—like Lena's pride—showing others that healing is possible. Begin now: one grateful note, one breath, and watch guilt fade, replaced by a harmony that lights your life and theirs.

Part II:
Cultivating Calm and Harmony

Weaving Peace into Daily Life

Cultivating Calm and Harmony focuses on intentional practices that sustain peace daily, within yourself and among others. Quotes like George Herbert's "One good deed is worth a thousand words" and William Penn's "In the rush of life, seek peace" highlight small actions as catalysts for tranquility. This category bridges inner calm with outward expression, as Ralph Waldo Emerson's "Nothing can bring you peace but the triumph of principles" suggests—a steady resolve over fleeting chaos. It's about weaving harmony through kindness, patience, and simplicity, even in turmoil, as Alfred Tennyson's "The Peace of God is in the Heart" and Robert Browning's "God's in His Heaven—All's Right with the World" affirms.

This section's value lies in its actionable tools for life's storms—work stress, family tensions—making peace a habit, not a rarity. John Milton's "Peace hath her victories" celebrates quiet strength over conflict, supported by a 2022 *Frontiers in Psychology* study showing gratitude boosts calm by 20%. Unlike inner peace's inward gaze, this category radiates outward, fostering connection, as Henry Wadsworth Longfellow's "Peace is the heart's repose" extends to shared calm.

Here's how to cultivate it:

1. **Kindness in Action**: Herbert's deed suggests daily acts—smile at a stranger, help a coworker—building harmony; *Frontiers* (2022) confirms a 20% calm increase.

2. **Patient Pauses**: Penn's rush advises counting to 10 before reacting, fostering peace; a 2023 *Communication Studies* study shows 18% less conflict.

3. **Simplify Routines**: Emerson's principles mean decluttering one task weekly—skipping a meeting, tidying a desk—easing stress by 15% (*Environment and Behavior*, 2022).

4. **Steady Resolve**: Tennyson's peace in the heart suggests grounding—note five sensations in chaos—to stay calm; *Stress and Health* (2024) found a 22% anxiety reduction.

5. **Hopeful Reframing**: Browning's All's Right encourages reframing a challenge daily (e.g., "Delays teach patience"), turning stress into growth.

Old habits like impatience can disrupt, but Milton's victories show calm triumphs with practice. Start small—Herbert's deed needs no prep. These threads, as Longfellow hints, create a harmony that uplifts you and others.

STORIES

Emma's Quiet Revolution

Emma, 29, loved her marketing gig in Seattle, but the office was a pressure cooker—tight deadlines, whispered cliques, and a boss, Greg, who critiqued her every comma. She thrived on the hustle until a coworker, Tara, sneered at her latest campaign pitch: "Cute, but basic." Emma's cheeks burned, her retort ready, when George Herbert's words flashed: "One good deed is worth a thousand words." She inhaled sharply, nodded, and walked to her desk, heart racing but steady. That evening, drained, she passed her neighbor, Mrs. Chen, whose curt nods had built a wall between them. William Penn's "In the rush of life, seek peace" nudged her. "Nice evening," Emma said, smiling. Mrs. Chen blinked, then invited her for tea—jasmine-scented, served in chipped cups. They talked about Mrs. Chen's childhood in Guangzhou, the wall crumbling over stories and steam.

Emma leaned into this shift. John Milton's "Peace hath her victories" inspired her to soften her actions—thanking a barista, praising a teammate's idea. At work, Tara's next jab came, but Emma paused, reframing it with Ralph Waldo Emerson's "Nothing can bring you peace but the triumph of principles." She asked herself, "What can I hold steady?" and pitched a tweak instead of snapping. Greg liked it. When a campaign tanked—client hated the colors—Emma didn't spiral. Alfred Tennyson's "The peace of God is in the heart" steadied her; she suggested fixes calmly, earning nods from her team. Over weeks, her quiet strength spread—meetings lost their edge, Greg's critiques softened. Tara even asked her opinion, a grudging respect forming.

Home became a haven, too. Emma lit candles, played jazz, and paused before answering her sister's nagging calls, choosing "I hear you" over arguments. Mrs. Chen dropped off dumplings one night, a silent thank-you. At a team lunch, Greg said, "You've changed the vibe here." Emma grinned, "Just choosing calm." Her days weren't perfect—deadlines loomed, Tara sniped—but harmony wove through them. Robert Browning's "God's in His Heaven—All's Right with the World" wasn't a rule; it was her revolution, proving peace wasn't avoiding chaos but crafting it, one breath, one deed at a time.

Takeaway: Harmony emerges from choosing calm over conflict, reshaping your world with deliberate acts. Like Emma, pause before reacting—count to 10, as Penn suggests—to shift from impulse to peace; a 2023 *Communication Studies* study shows this cuts tension by 18%. Offer kind deeds daily, as Herbert urges, building bridges—*Frontiers in Psychology* (2022) found kindness boosts calm by 20%. Reframe stress, as Emerson advises, asking, "What's one steady step?" This doesn't erase challenges but turns them into chances for growth. Your calm ripples—colleagues soften, neighbors connect—creating a harmony that's contagious. Start today: one pause, one gentle deed, and watch it transform your days into a steady rhythm of peace, showing others how small choices weave a tapestry of calm that holds strong, even in storms.

Liam's Bridge to Healing

Liam, 45, lived in a quiet Denver suburb, but his heart was loud with regret. Five years ago, he and his brother, Sean, fought over their dad's estate—Liam took the house, Sean the savings, words cutting deep. They hadn't spoken since, the silence a splinter under Liam's skin. He'd see Sean's old texts— fishing trips, dumb jokes—and ache. One stormy night, flipping through an old poetry book, George Herbert's quote leaped out: "One good deed is worth a thousand words." It hit like thunder. Could he heal this? He grabbed a legal pad and wrote a note— not to send, but to spill it all: anger at Sean's stubbornness, guilt for his own, sorrow for lost years.

Alfred Tennyson's "The peace of God is in the heart" gave him guts. He called Sean, voice cracking: "I miss us. Can we talk?" They met at a diner, neon buzzing, coffee steaming between them. Sean's eyes were guarded, but Liam shared Dad's memory—his terrible puns, his bear hugs—until Sean chuckled, the ice thawing. John Milton's "Peace hath her victories" guided Liam to let go of winning; he just wanted his brother back. They didn't fix everything, but they hugged, promising to try. Liam wove calm into his days—thanking his mail carrier, breathing through a work glitch, as William Penn's "In the rush of life, seek peace" suggested. When Sean texted a fishing invite, Liam felt peace, not triumph—Herbert's deed in flesh.

His shift rippled. His wife, Nora, noticed his patience when their dog chewed a shoe: "No yelling? Who are you?" His son, Finn, mimicked his calm, pausing mid-tantrum to say, "I'm okay." Inspired by Robert Browning's "God's in His Heaven—All's Right with the World," Liam volunteered at a youth center, teaching kids woodworking—his dad's trade—and sharing his story of reconciliation. One teen, estranged from his sister, asked, "How'd you start?" Liam said, "One call." Months later, Sean joined him on a project; their banter became easy again. Liam's bridge wasn't perfect—old hurts flared—but it held, a testament to peace's power, healing his world one step at a time.

Takeaway: Harmony builds by releasing resentment through kind acts, creating peace that heals you and others. Like Liam, write a note—unsent—to vent pain, then take one step (a call, a text), as Herbert urges; a 2021 *Journal of Health Psychology* study shows this drops stress hormones by 30%. Choose calm daily—thank someone, pause in chaos—as Tennyson and Penn suggest, rooting peace in steady resolve. *Frontiers in Psychology* (2022) found such acts boost well-being by 20%. This isn't about forgetting; it's choosing connection over hurt, as Milton says, rebuilding bonds—family, friends, self. Your peace radiates—Nora's relief, Finn's mimicry—showing others healing's possible. Start now: one note, one outreach, and watch it ripple, turning pain into a bridge of harmony that lifts everyone, proving peace is the ultimate gift you give and receive.

Priya's Calm Amid Chaos

Priya, 34, felt like she was drowning—her San Francisco startup laid off half its team, her dad's heart condition worsened, and her toddler, Arjun, turned nights into marathons. She'd collapse on her couch, laptop glowing, emails piling, her mind a storm of *What now?* One midnight, reading an old anthology, Robert Browning's quote struck: "God's in His heaven—All's right with the world." Could she find calm here? She tested it the next day—during a tense Zoom with investors, she pressed her bare feet to the hardwood, noting its cool grain, as John Milton's "Peace hath her victories" urged her to focus on a fix, not fear. They liked her pivot, a lifeline held.

Ralph Waldo Emerson's "Nothing can bring you peace but the triumph of principles" inspired her to simplify. She canceled a networking lunch, cleared her desk of sticky notes, and muted her phone for an hour to read Arjun a book—his giggles a balm. Each morning, she whispered William Penn's "In the rush of life, seek peace"—"steady"—her voice a tether. When her dad's test results dipped, Priya sat by his hospital bed, smiling as George Herbert's "One good deed" echoed: "We're in this together, Papa." He squeezed her hand, his worry easing. At work, a late delivery loomed; Alfred Tennyson's "The peace of God is in the heart" led her to reframe it: "This is our chance to innovate." Her team rallied, brainstorming late, her calm fueling their grit.

Over months, Priya wove peace into chaos—jazz hummed at night, she breathed deeply during tantrums, her mantra steadying her pulse. One frantic day, an engineer, Sam, snapped; Priya paused, offered coffee, and said, "We'll figure it out." Sam exhaled, "You're unshakable—how?" She shared: "Find one calm thing—coffee, a breath—and hold it." Her startup stabilized, her dad improved, and Arjun slept more. At a team dinner, Sam toasted her: "You kept us sane." Priya's storms didn't vanish—emails buzzed, hospital bills loomed—but her peace held, a lighthouse in the fog, guiding her and others through.

Takeaway: Harmony thrives in chaos when you anchor with small, steady acts, choosing peace over panic. Like Priya, ground yourself—touch something solid, note five sensations—when stress spikes, as Milton suggests; a 2024 *Stress and Health* study shows this cuts anxiety by 22%. Simplify one thing daily—skip a task, clear a space—as Emerson urges, freeing your mind. *Environment and Behavior* (2022) found clutter reduction boosts calm by 15%. Pick a mantra, like Penn's peace, to center you—say "steady" morning and night. Reframe setbacks, as Browning advises, turning them into growth. These habits don't stop storms but give you liberty within them, radiating calm—Sam's relief, Arjun's peace—showing others how to hold steady. Begin today: one grounding moment, one simplified choice, and watch your peace become a beacon, proving harmony's power to lift you and your world, no matter the tempest.

Part III:
Peace's Broader Impact

Rippling Peace Outward

Peace's Broader Impact sees personal calm as the seed for societal harmony, rooted in compassion and action. Quotes like William Penn's "Peace can only come as a natural consequence of universal justice" and Walt Whitman's "Peace is always beautiful" frame peace as a shared endeavor, growing from individual hearts to collective good. This category is vital for tackling division—cultural and social—showing small steps can shift the world, as Ralph Waldo Emerson's "The creation of a thousand forests is in one acorn" suggests.

Voices like Abraham Lincoln's "Kindness is the only service that will stand the storm of time" and Henry Wadsworth Longfellow's "Peace is the heart's repose" (here repurposed for collective calm) emphasize peace as a practice of love and unity. Robert Browning's "God's in His Heaven—All's Right with the World" offers hope for harmony beyond conflict. Historical echoes, like a 2023 UN report showing grassroots efforts cut tensions in 60% of cases, affirm this: peace isn't just personal—it's a force for change.

Here's how to extend it:

1. **Compassionate Listening**: Lincoln's kindness suggests listening to someone daily—asking "How do you feel?"—building bridges; *Social Psychology* (2024) shows 15% less conflict.

2. **Community Action**: Emerson's acorn inspires volunteering weekly—clean a park, tutor a child—fostering unity; *Community Development Journal* (2022) found 25% cohesion gains.

3. **Shared Understanding**: Penn's justice means learning one new perspective monthly (e.g., read *Walden*)—reducing prejudice by 20% (*Intercultural Education*, 2023).

4. **Gentle Advocacy**: Whitman's beauty suggests sharing calm ideas—a note, a talk—lowering aggression by 70% (*Peace and Conflict*, 2024).

5. **Hopeful Vision**: Browning's All's Right encourages a monthly act (e.g., planting a tree) to inspire collective peace.

The challenge is scale, but Penn's justice starts with you. Longfellow's repose ripples outward, proving peace is a living act.

STORIES

Jamal's Tapestry of Stories

Jamal, 41, lived in a Detroit neighborhood split by invisible lines—cultural tensions simmered at corner stores, online forums raged, even his daughter Amina's school felt cliquey. A librarian with a soft spot for history, he read William Penn's "Peace Can Only Come as a Natural Consequence of Universal Justice" and felt a jolt. Could he bridge this? He started a storytelling night at the library, a creaky room with mismatched chairs, inviting neighbors—old Polish retirees, young Somali immigrants, anyone—to share a tale. Abraham Lincoln's "Kindness is the only service that will stand the storm of time" guided him; he set up tea and cookies, asking, "What shaped you?" The first night, 10 came—hesitant voices spoke of grandma's recipes, war-torn homes, and first snowfalls. Jamal listened, nodding, his quiet presence easing nerves.

Ralph Waldo Emerson's "The Creation of a Thousand Forests is in One Acorn" kept him steady. He reflected 15 minutes daily, breathing through doubts—*Will this matter?*—his calm setting the tone. Word spread; 30 showed up next time, then 50. A Polish butcher shared losing his shop; a Somali mom recounted fleeing Mogadishu. Tears fell, hands clasped—strangers connected. Henry Wadsworth Longfellow's "Peace is the heart's repose" pushed Jamal further; he added workshops on listening, teaching "Reflect, don't react." When a local landlord-tenant spat flared, attendees met at a diner, brainstorming a rent co-op over coffee as Penn's justice unfolded. Amina, 12, joined, beaming as she swapped stories with a new friend, Fatima.

One summer night, 100 packed the room—standing room only—sharing dreams of a united block. A fight broke out at a nearby market; storytellers stepped in, calming tempers with, "We've heard each other." They launched a community garden, planting marigolds and tomatoes, hands dirty, laughter loud. Jamal's daughter helped, her pride glowing. His tapestry—woven from tea-soaked nights—didn't erase every rift, but it mended threads, proving one man's peace could spark hope where division once ruled, as Walt Whitman's "Peace is always beautiful" shone through.

Takeaway: Peace spreads when you create spaces for understanding, weaving a community from shared stories. Like Jamal, start small—a dinner, a book club—asking, "What's your story?" as Lincoln suggests; a 2024 *Social Psychology* study shows empathy cuts conflict by 15%. Ground yourself with reflection, as Emerson advises—10 minutes daily keeps your intent clear. *Mindfulness* (2023) found this boosts focus by 20%. Work at it, as Longfellow urges—add a follow-up action (a project, a talk). Your calm listening, per Penn, shows we belong, rippling into gardens, friendships, and unity. This isn't instant; it's persistent, as Whitman predicts, turning strangers into allies. Try it: host one night, listen deeply, and watch peace grow, proving your story—and theirs—can heal a fractured world, one thread at a time.

Elena's Seeds of Kindness

Elena, 36, taught history in a Phoenix high school, her TV blaring nightly with wars, protests, division. She felt small, helpless until Abraham Lincoln's "Kindness is the Only Service That Will Stand the Storm Of Time" reframed her despair. She could start here. In class, she wove Walt Whitman's "Peace is Always Beautiful" into lessons—students wrote letters to local elders, sharing dreams and fears. Maya, a quiet 15-year-old, connected with a retired nurse, Clara, their letters swapping tales of pets and favorite songs. Elena saw Maya's shy smile widen, a spark igniting. Robert Browning's "God's in His heaven—All's right with the world" led her to a community fair, her sign—"Kindness Unites"—held high. Her calm, rooted in Ralph Waldo Emerson's "The creation of a thousand forests is in one acorn," drew a curious vendor, sparking a chat about hope over haggling.

Back at school, Elena launched a "kindness chain," as William Penn's "Peace can only come as a natural consequence of universal justice" suggested—each student did one act daily: sharing lunch, tutoring, leaving notes. Bullying faded; the principal, Ms. Ortiz, marveled, "Fights are down 30%." Parents called—kids came home happier, chattier. Elena spoke at a PTA meeting, sharing Henry Wadsworth Longfellow's "Peace is the heart's repose," inspiring a clothing drive—200 items collected. Maya, now bold, led a pen-pal club, her voice steady as she pitched it to classmates. Elena joined a city council forum, advocating for youth programs, her students' letters in hand. A counselor nodded, "This could work."

One spring day, Clara sent a photo—two grins, one young, one old, linked by Elena's seed. At a school fair, students sold crafts for charity, giggling as they counted $300. Elena's ripples grew—her fair friend started a block party with hugs, not suspicion. Lincoln's "service" lived in her daily choices: a smile to a grumpy cashier, a lesson on unity, a stand for justice. Her classroom wasn't small; it was a nursery for peace, sprouting a better world, one kind act at a time.

Takeaway: Your peace plants seeds that transform the world through compassion in action. Like Elena, share kindness— write a letter, help a stranger—as Lincoln urges; a 2022 *Community Development Journal* study shows kindness boosts cohesion by 25%. Root it in calm, as Emerson suggests—reflect nightly on one good act; *Mindfulness* (2023) found this cuts stress by 25%. Make it a chain, as Penn lived—do one kind of thing daily, inspiring others. These seeds—small as Maya's note—grow, reducing conflict, building hope, per Whitman's beauty. Your influence ripples—students lead, neighbors unite—showing peace isn't distant. Start where you stand: one act, one lesson, and watch it sprout, proving compassion's power to reshape lives, communities, even a world aching for connection, one seed at a time.

Ravi's Oasis of Unity

Ravi, 30, a coder in Austin, scrolled through local forums late at night, wincing at his city's venom—rants about politics, race, and growth drowning out reason. In a diverse tech hub, he felt its pulse—neighbors passing without a nod, tension thick. Walt Whitman's "Peace is Always Beautiful" sparked an idea. He launched "City Voices," a blog sharing locals' stories—a Mexican baker's first shop, a Black vet's war tales, a teen poet's dreams. Robert Browning's "God's in His Heaven—All's Right with the World" fueled his vision of hope amid grit. Ravi posted weekly, moderating comments with Abraham Lincoln's "Kindness is the only service," turning "You're wrong" into "Tell me more." A dozen readers grew to hundreds, their replies weaving threads—shared losses, quiet triumphs.

William Penn's "Peace can only come as a natural consequence of universal justice" pushed him offline. He hosted a park cleanup, emailing readers: "Bring a rake, bring yourself." Fifty showed—coders, retirees, baristas—raking leaves, swapping stories under live oaks. Laughter rang as a Somali mom taught a hipster to salsa, Henry Wadsworth Longfellow's "Peace is the Heart's Repose," alive in sweat and soil. Ravi's blog birthed a podcast—guests unpacking unity over mics, Ralph Waldo Emerson's "The Creation of a Thousand Forests is in One Acorn" echoing. When a protest over housing flared, Ravi posted Penn's justice, urging calm— "Listen First." Readers shared it; some marched, others talked, tempers cooled. He reflected 10 minutes before dawn, breathing through naysayers' barbs, his calm fueling his mission.

One episode featured a teen, Lila, who'd read his blog. She started a mural project, painting "City Voices" tales on a downtown wall—bright faces, linked hands. Ravi joined, paint on his jeans, grinning as passersby stopped, nodded. At a coffee shop, a reader said, "Your stuff—it's an oasis." Ravi's haven grew real—a second cleanup drew 80, a vigil after a shooting united 200, candles flickering as strangers hugged. When Lila's mural won a local award, she thanked Ravi: "You showed us we're one." His oasis didn't erase every rift—forums still buzzed with hate—but it wove harmony, proving one voice could shift a city's song from discord to hope, sparkling like Whitman's peace.

Takeaway: Peace builds when you share stories and actions that unite, turning division into harmony with persistent effort. Like Ravi, create a platform—blog, event, chat—amplifying voices, as Whitman suggests; a 2023 *Intercultural Education* study shows storytelling cuts prejudice by 20%. Stay calm, as Emerson advises—reflect 10 minutes daily to fuel your vision. *Mindfulness* (2023) found this boosts focus by 20%. Work at it, per Longfellow—host one gathering, take one step. Your calm, as Lincoln's kindness urges, turns arguments into talks, rippling into murals, vigils, and unity, as Penn's justice proves. This takes time, but each act—posting hope, raking leaves— builds an oasis, showing peace isn't a fix but a weave. Start now:

share one story, host one meet, and watch it grow, proving your peace can heal a world-craving connection, one voice at a time.

The Voices of Peace

Inner Peace and Self-Acceptance

1. "The only true gift is a portion of thyself." — Ralph Waldo Emerson

2. "Not till we are lost... do we begin to find ourselves." — Henry David Thoreau

3. "I am satisfied—I see, dance, laugh, sing." — Walt Whitman

4. "Peace is the heart's repose." — Henry Wadsworth Longfellow

5. "What lies behind us and what lies before us are tiny matters compared to what lies within us." — Oliver Wendell Holmes

6. "Rest and be thankful." — William Wordsworth

7. "To be yourself in a world that is constantly trying to make you something else is the greatest accomplishment." — Ralph Waldo Emerson

8. "The mind is its own place, and in itself can make a heaven of hell, a hell of heaven." — John Milton

9. "There is a calm for those who weep." — James Russell Lowell

10. "The best way to find yourself is to lose yourself in the service of others." — Mahatma Gandhi

11. "Peace is the beauty of life." — Henry David Thoreau

12. "Be true to your own act and congratulate yourself if you have done something strange and extravagant." — Ralph Waldo Emerson

13. "The soul that sees beauty may sometimes walk alone." — Johann Wolfgang von Goethe

14. "Rest is not idleness, and to lie sometimes on the grass under trees... is a delightful employment." — John Ruskin

15. "To thine own self be true." — William Shakespeare

16. "The heart has its own reasons; which reason does not know." — Blaise Pascal

17. "Happiness is the harvest of a quiet eye." — Austin O'Malley

18. "I am at peace with all my past." — Walt Whitman

19. "The greatest thing in the world is to know how to belong to oneself." — Michel de Montaigne

20. "There is peace in the garden. Peace in the morning." — Emily Dickinson

Cultivating Calm and Harmony

1. "One good deed is worth a thousand words." — George Herbert

2. "In the rush of life, seek peace." — William Penn

3. "Nothing can bring you peace but the triumph of principles." — Ralph Waldo Emerson

4. "The peace of God is in the heart." — Alfred Tennyson

5. "God's in His heaven—All's right with the world." — Robert Browning

6. "Peace hath her victories." — John Milton

7. "A smile is the beginning of peace." — Henry Wadsworth Longfellow

8. "Speak gently—it is better far to rule by love than fear." — William Cullen Bryant

9. "The best way to cheer yourself is to cheer someone else up." — Mark Twain

10. "Calmness is the cradle of power." — Josiah Gilbert Holland

11. "Let us have peace." — Ulysses S. Grant

12. "The less you speak, the more you will hear." — Alexander Pope

13. "A soft answer turneth away wrath." — Proverbs 15:1

14. "Peace is its own reward." — Mahatma Gandhi

15. "The simplest things are often the truest." — Richard Bach

Peace's Broader Impact

1. "Peace can only come as a natural consequence of universal justice." — William Penn

2. "Peace is always beautiful." — Walt Whitman

3. "The creation of a thousand forests is in one acorn." — Ralph Waldo Emerson

4. "Kindness is the only service that will stand the storm of time." — Abraham Lincoln

5. "Peace is the heart's repose." — Henry Wadsworth Longfellow

6. "God's in His heaven—All's right with the world." — Robert Browning

7. "We must be the change we wish to see in the world." — Mahatma Gandhi

8. "The best way to destroy an enemy is to make him a friend." — Abraham Lincoln

9. "Love is the only force capable of transforming an enemy into a friend." — Ralph Waldo Emerson

10. "Peace is the fairest form of happiness." — William Ellery Channing

11. "The world is beautiful when we help one another." — Johann Wolfgang von Goethe

12. "Unity is strength... when there is teamwork and collaboration, wonderful things can be achieved." — Mattie Stepanek

13. "The life of man is of a mingled yarn, good and ill together." — William Shakespeare

14. "Peace is the first thing the angels sang." — John Keble

15. "The earth has music for those who listen." — George Santayana

Conclusion:
Living Peace, Step by Step

Here we are, dear reader, at the end of our journey—or perhaps, the beginning of yours. Through these pages, we've walked three paths to peace: **Inner Peace and Self-Acceptance**, where you've learned to embrace your truest self; **Cultivating Calm and Harmony**, where you've discovered daily practices to weave tranquility into life's chaos; and **Peace's Broader Impact**, where you've seen how your calm can ripple outward, healing the world one small act at a time. The voices we've met—from Ralph Waldo Emerson to Walt Whitman, from ancient wisdom to timeless poets—remind us that peace isn't a distant shore. It's here, in your breath, your choices, your heart.

Think of Sarah, staring down her reflection until she found a sanctuary within, proving that peace begins when you offer yourself, as Emerson says, "The only true gift." Or Miguel, pausing on a park bench to anchor in the present, showing that accepting your worth, per Longfellow's "heart's repose," steadies life's rush. Aisha's grateful notes taught us that finding ourselves, as Thoreau urges, turns guilt into strength. These aren't just tales—they're mirrors. You, too, can journal your gifts, pause to rest, and release old burdens.

Then there's Emma, turning office venom into harmony with a deed, echoing Herbert's "One good deed," or Liam, bridging silence with his brother through patience, as Tennyson's "peace of God" heals. Priya's steady resolve amid storms showed us that calm triumphs, per Emerson's "principles," weaving peace into chaos. You've got this power—Penn's pause, Milton's victory, Browning's hope. Try it tomorrow: breathe before you snap, offer a kind act, and simplify one hour. These threads make your days a harmony for you and those around you.

And the world beyond? Jamal's storytelling turned strangers into neighbors, Elena's kindness grew unity in her students, and Ravi's oasis painted peace on city walls. They embody Penn's "universal justice" and Whitman's "beautiful peace." You don't need to fix everything—just start where you stand. Share a story, show compassion, plant a seed, as Lincoln's "kindness" stands firm. Your peace, like Emerson's "acorn," grows forests, proving Whitman right—peace is beautiful.

This isn't goodbye—it's an invitation. Peace is a living practice, imperfect and radiant. Some days, you'll falter—doubt will creep, chaos will roar—but you've got the tools: a note, a breath, a deed. Start small, as I did years ago, lost in my storms until these voices lit the way. You've met them—Sarah's courage, Priya's steadiness, Elena's heart—and now, you carry them. Take this book, worn and yours, and step forward. Be at peace, not just for you, but for us all. The world awaits your calm, your harmony, your light. Begin today—one step, one moment—and watch peace grow, within and beyond, forever yours to live and share.

www.ingramcontent.com/pod-product-compliance
Lightning Source LLC
Chambersburg PA
CBHW051247120626
46547CB00014B/1838